Ransom Reading Stars

Powerboat Race
by Stephen Rickard

Published by Ransom Publishing Ltd.
Unit 7, Brocklands Farm, West Meon, Hampshire GU32 1JN, UK
www.ransom.co.uk

ISBN 978 178591 838 4
First published in 2010
This revised edition published 2019

Copyright © 2019 Ransom Publishing Ltd.
Text copyright © 2019 Ransom Publishing Ltd.
All photographs copyright © 2008 Powerboat P1 Management Ltd. except Nigel wearing helmet - copyright © 2009 Janet Wilson

Special thanks to Janet Wilson and Nigel Hook for all their help.

A CIP catalogue record of this book is available from the British Library.

All rights reserved. No part of this publication may be reproduced, stored in a retrieval system, or transmitted, in any form or by any means, electronic, mechanical, photocopying, recording or otherwise, without the prior permission of the publishers.

The right of Stephen Rickard to be identified as the author of this Work has been asserted by him in accordance with sections 77 and 78 of the Copyright, Design and Patents Act 1988.

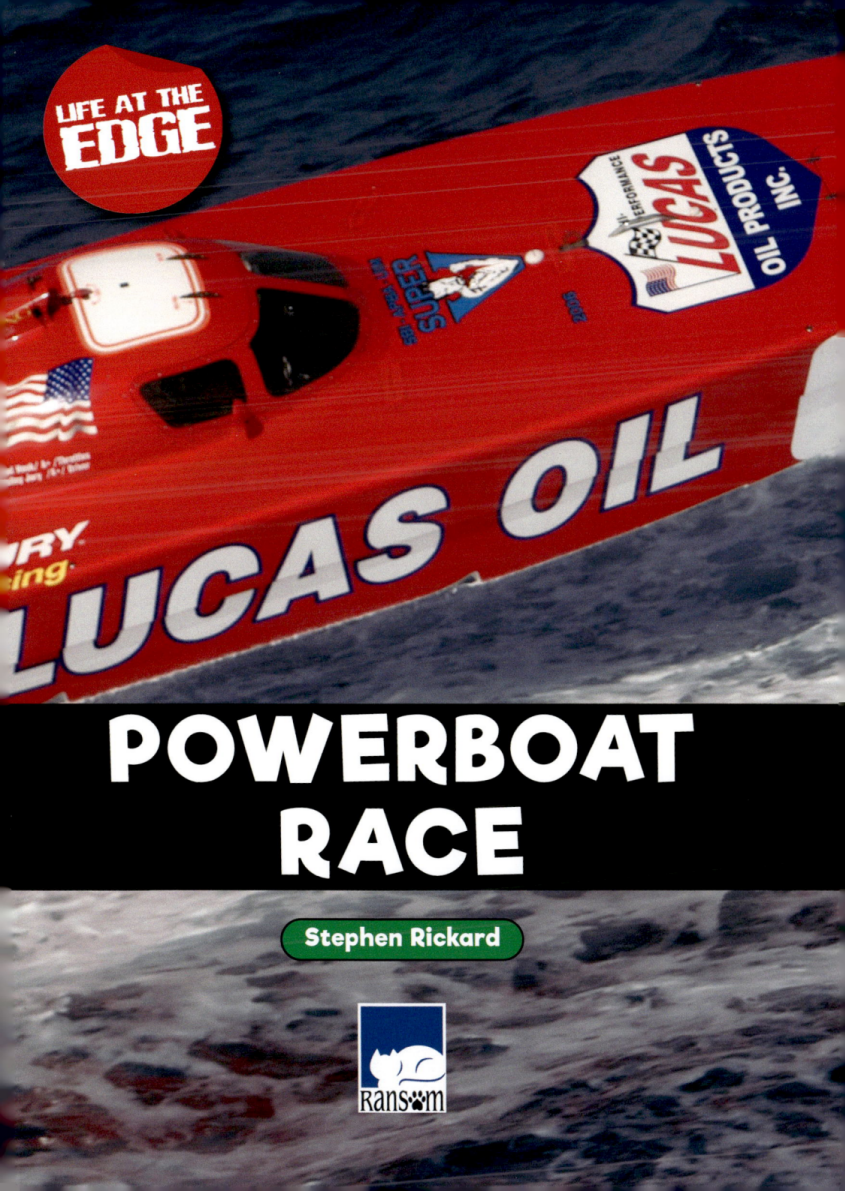

Hull.
Made of carbon fibre. Carbon fibre is very light and very strong.

Cockpit.
The cockpit has two seats, one for the throttle man and one for the driver.

Powerboat Data

Length:	12.3 metres
Height:	2.0 metres
Engines:	Two. 750 horse power each
Top speed:	193 km/hour (120 mph)

This is Shelley Jory. She races with me.

I am the throttle man. I control the speed of the boat. Shelley is the driver. She steers the boat.

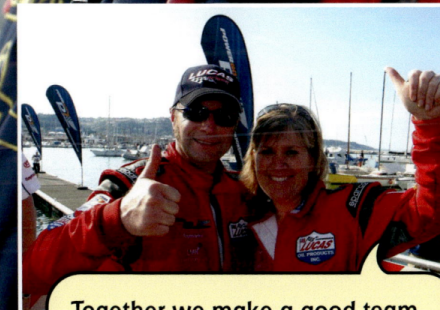

Together we make a good team.

Today is race day. It is a Powerboat P1 Grand Prix.

At every race, we have two pits. These are the dry pits. They are on land.

This is our race boat. It is very heavy. It weighs more than 5,000 kg.

We use a big crane to lift it into the water.

Can you see the propellors at the back? The boat has two engines and two propellors.

Each engine can give out 750 horse power. This boat is three times more powerful than a Ferrari car.

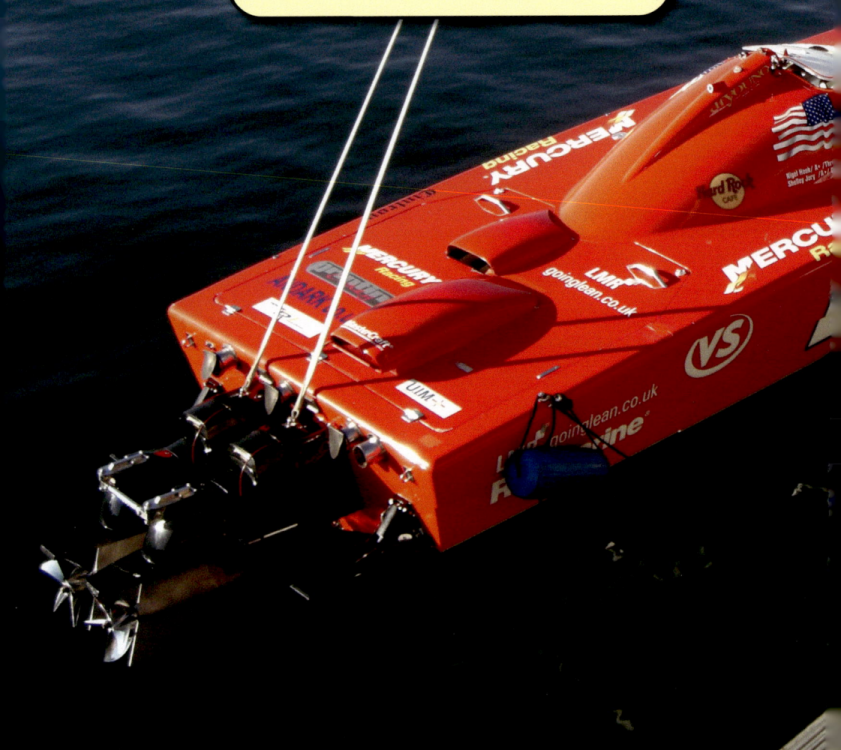

Then we go back to work.

Shelley and I think about the race. How will we win?

The race is 128 kilometres long.

The racecourse is shown with floating markers. One lap of the course is 8 kilometres, so we need to do 16 laps of the course to finish the race.

Our powerboat is travelling at 185 kilometres per hour. This is nearly top speed.

The boat hits the waves hard. This makes it very bumpy and dangerous, and my body gets jolted by the waves. It's a good job that we are both strapped in tight.

We must be careful too. The boat might capsize.

The fans watch from the shore. They get to see all of the race.

It is very noisy in the cockpit.

Shelley and I have radios in our helmets, so that we can talk to each other during the race.

Now we are close to the boat in front of us. We are fighting for second place.

We find the best line. This is the shortest and quickest way to the finish.

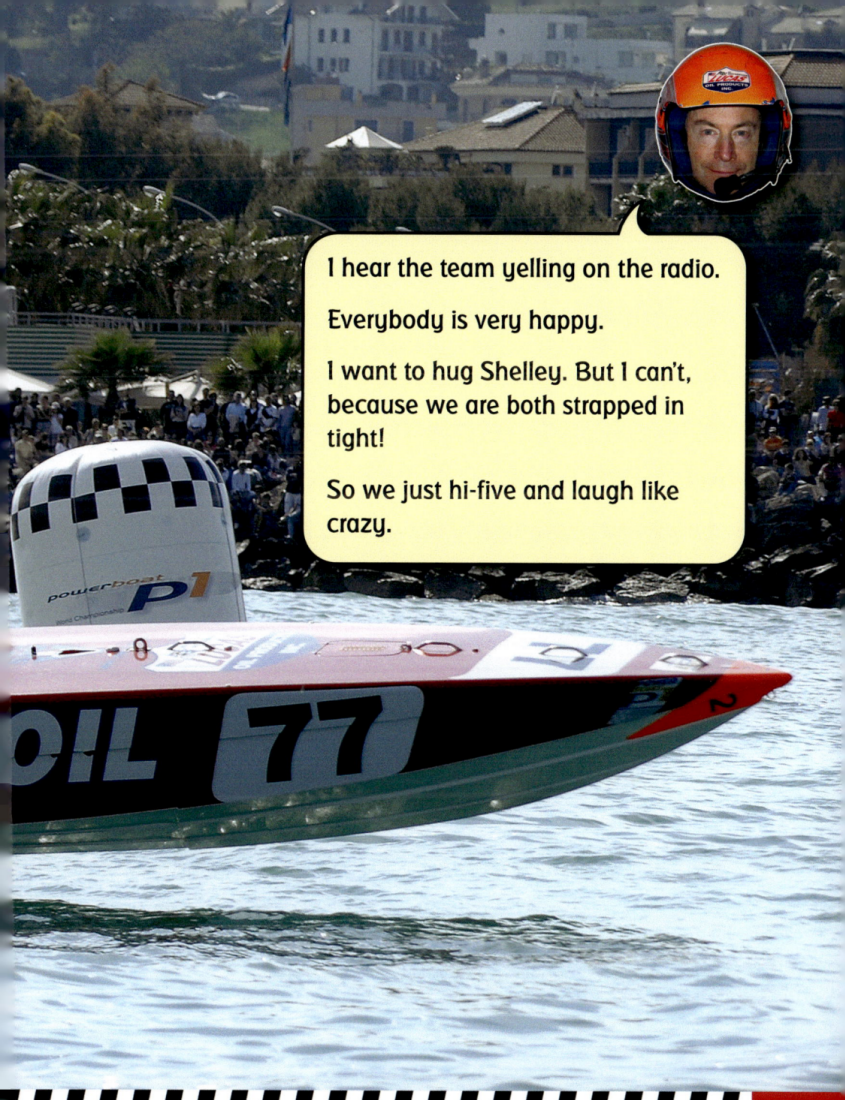

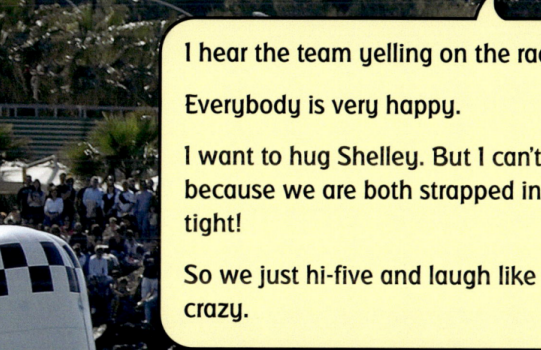

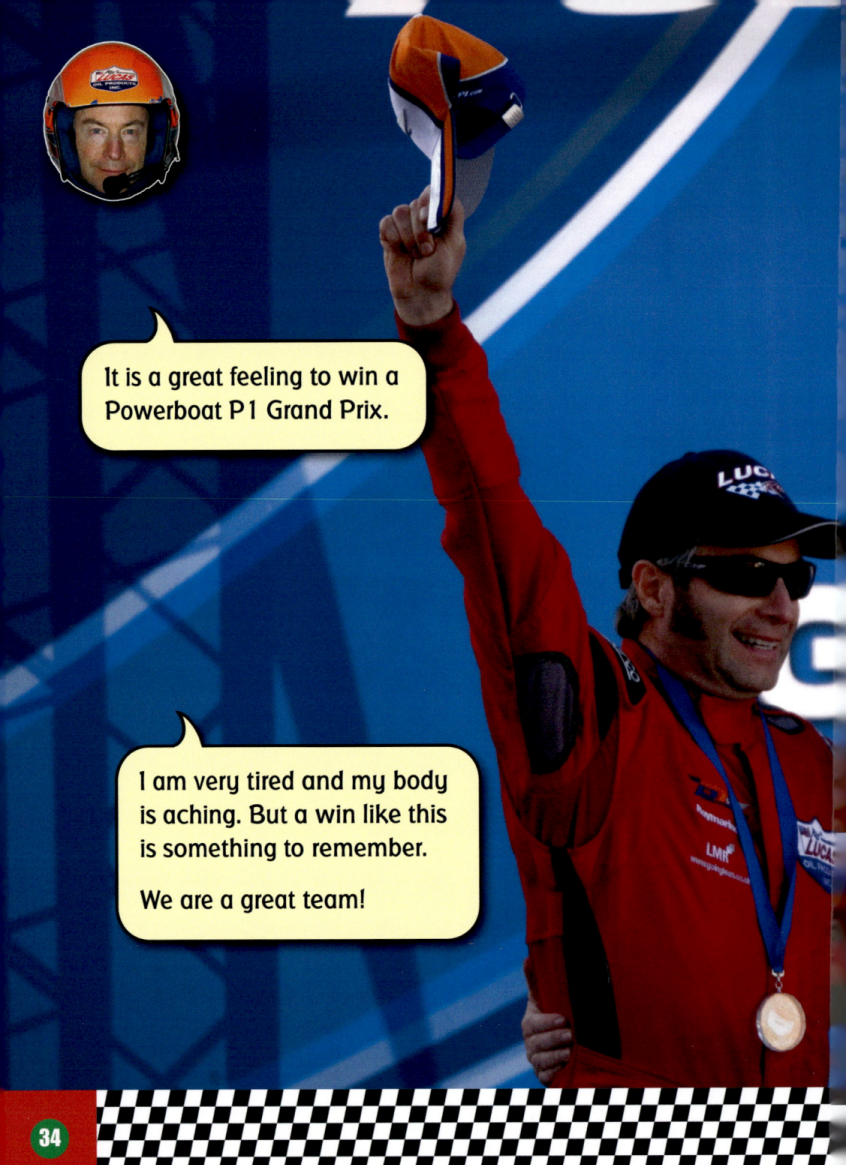

Jargon Buster (word list)

autograph
capsize
carbon fibre
cockpit
concentrate
course
driver
dry pits
engine
engine bay
Evolution P1
Grand Prix
hatch
helmet

horse power
interview
kilometre
lap
offshore
P1
pilot
powerboat
propellor
racecourse
radio
rotate
throttle man
wet pits